SCHIRMER'S LIBRARY
OF MUSICAL CLASSICS

Vol. 1797

WOLFGANG AMADEUS MOZART

Six Viennese Sonatinas
For the Piano

Edited by
JOSEPH PROSTAKOFF

G. SCHIRMER, Inc.

DISTRIBUTED BY

HAL•LEONARD®
CORPORATION
7777 W. BLUEMOUND RD. P.O. BOX 13819 MILWAUKEE, WI 53213

FOREWORD

The piano pieces which have become widely known as *Six Viennese Sonatinas* are transcriptions of selected movements from Five Divertimenti (Serenades) for two clarinets and bassoon (Köchel-Einstein Catalogue 439b), composed by Mozart in Vienna, approximately in 1783. The first arrangement for the piano was made by an anonymous transcriber and printed by the Viennese music publisher, Artaria, shortly after Mozart's death.

The quality of this transcription, on which all subsequent publications of these pieces seem to have been based, is very uneven. Its serious flaws become immediately and glaringly apparent on comparison with the original instrumental version. Although some sections were transcribed faithfully and with insight, there were many changes made elsewhere which simply cannot be justified by the presumed intention to make the music more pianistic or easier to play. Changes in harmony were made, all too often transforming a striking and bold progression into a commonplace one. Innumerable cuts, from one to as many as fifty-one bars, altered and distorted the form.

Even Mozart's main melodic line was not always safe from capricious meddling and the individual and graceful lines of the ensemble were not preserved where this could be done easily. The ebb and flow of tonal motion was changed without regard to its presence in the original. Sustained whole notes became quarter-notes. On the other hand, a quickening from eighth-notes to sixteenths has at times been ignored, even in places where no difficulty existed. The intention of the composer was often blunted and sometimes lost. Finally, there is present in many places, a somewhat thick and unresonant tonal mixture, due to a combination of too low a register with a high treble, which cannot be found either in the original or in the compositions written directly for the piano by Mozart.

Consequently, it seemed essential to provide for this edition a new version. While the order of the movements in each sonatina was kept in the sequence which has become familiar, the sections which had been cut out were restored. Some places were transcribed anew and in all matters of melody, harmony and rhythmic flow the original instrumental version was followed in order to restore, in each separate piece, the original idea of Mozart.

J. P.

Sonatina I

W. A. Mozart
Edited by Joseph Prostakoff

Menuetto

Allegretto

Adagio

Rondo

Allegretto

Sonatina II

Menuetto

Allegretto

Adagio

Rondo
Allegro

Ossia

Sonatina III

Trio

Fine

Menuetto da capo

Rondo
Allegro

*Ossia

etc.

Repeat *p*

Repeat *p*

Sonatina IV

Romanze
Andante

Menuetto
Allegretto

Trio

Rondo

Allegro assai

Sonatina V

Menuetto

Allegretto

Polonaise

Sonatina VI

Menuetto

Allegretto

Trio

Ossia

Ossia

Menuetto da capo

Adagio

p dolce

Finale

Allegro

*Although F♯ may be played here, the original has F♮ at this point.